WORLD SERIES CHAMPIONS

CHICAGO WHITE SOX

Published by Creative Education
P.O. Box 227, Mankato, Minnesota 56002
Creative Education is an imprint of The Creative Company
www.thecreativecompany.us

Design and production by Blue Design
Printed in the United States of America

Photographs by Corbis (Bettmann), Getty Images (Brian Bahr, Al Bello, Richard Cummins, Jonathan Daniel, Diamond Images/Getty Images, John Grieshop/MLB Photos, Brad Mangin/MLB Photos, Francis Miller//Time Life Pictures, National Baseball Hall of Fame Library/MLB Photos, Rich Pilling/MLB Photos, Robert Riger Collection, Mark Rucker/Transcendental Graphics, Donald F. Smith//Time Life Pictures, Three Lions, Ron Vesely/MLB Photos)

Library of Congress Cataloging-in-Publication Data

Frisch, Aaron.
Chicago White Sox / by Aaron Frisch.
p. cm. — (World Series champions)
Includes index.
ISBN 978-1-58341-696-9
1. Chicago White Sox (Baseball team)—History—Juvenile literature. I. Title. II. Series.

GV875.C58F745 2009
796.357'640977311—dc22   2008003768

First edition
9 8 7 6 5 4 3 2 1

Cover: Outfielder Jermaine Dye (top), 1958 White Sox (bottom)
Page 1: Second baseman Geoff Blum
Page 3: Catcher A. J. Pierzynski

WORLD SERIES CHAMPIONS

CHICAGO WHITE SOX

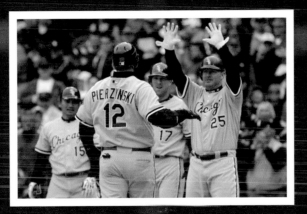

AARON FRISCH

CREATIVE EDUCATION

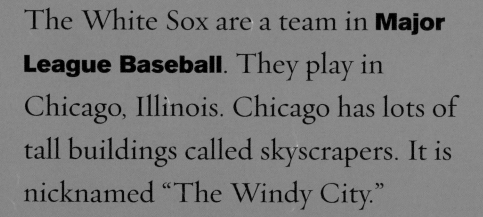

The White Sox are a team in **Major League Baseball**. They play in Chicago, Illinois. Chicago has lots of tall buildings called skyscrapers. It is nicknamed "The Windy City."

5

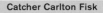
Catcher Carlton Fisk

The White Sox have a stadium called U.S. Cellular Field. Their uniforms are white and black. The White Sox play lots of games against teams called the Indians, Royals, Tigers, and Twins.

PITCHER
ED WALSH

8

PITCHER
CLARK GRIFFITH

The White Sox started playing in 1900. In 1901, they won the **pennant**. In 1906, they won their first World Series! They beat another Chicago team called the Cubs.

The White Sox soon got a good outfielder named Joe Jackson. People called him "Shoeless Joe." He helped Chicago win the World Series in 1917. The White Sox played in the World Series again two years later. But this time they lost.

OUTFIELDER

JOE JACKSON

1919 White Sox

13

LUIS APARICIO

Chicago got more good players after that. Eddie Collins played great defense at second base. But the White Sox lost a lot of games. In the 1950s, they got some fast players. Fans called them the "Go-Go Sox"!

SECOND BASEMAN
EDDIE COLLINS

15

SECOND BASEMAN
NELLIE FOX

16

PITCHER
WILBUR WOOD

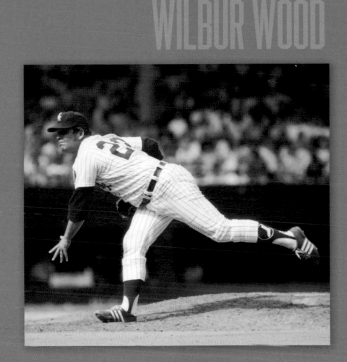

Second baseman Nellie Fox helped
the White Sox get to the World
Series in 1959. But they lost.
Pitcher Wilbur Wood threw great
knuckleballs in the 1970s. But
Chicago was not as good anymore.

17

Pitcher Jack McDowell

In the 1990s, the White Sox
were an exciting team. Strong
first baseman Frank Thomas
blasted a lot of home runs.
Pitcher Jack McDowell struck
out many batters. The White Sox
made the **playoffs** in 1993.

FIRST BASEMAN
FRANK THOMAS

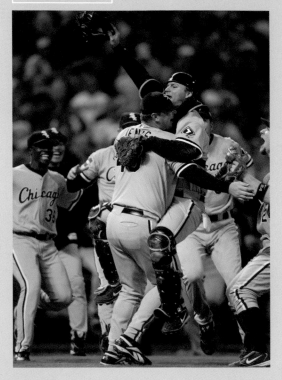
2005 World Series

The White Sox got to the playoffs
again in 2005. They won 11 games
and lost only 1. Pitcher Jon Garland
helped the White Sox beat a team
called the Astros in the World
Series! It was Chicago's first world
championship in 88 years.

PITCHER
JON GARLAND

21

FIRST BASEMAN
PAUL KONERKO

22

Paul Konerko was another good White Sox player. He was a first baseman who bashed lots of home runs. Chicago fans hope that today's White Sox will win the World Series again soon!

GLOSSARY

knuckleballs — pitches that don't spin; the ball goes slow but moves around in strange ways

Major League Baseball — a group of 30 baseball teams that play against each other; major-league teams have the best players in the world

pennant — the championship of a baseball league

playoffs — games that are played after the season to see which team is the champion

WHITE SOX FACTS

Team colors: white and black

First home stadium: South Side Park

Home stadium today: U.S. Cellular Field

League/Division: American League, Central Division

First season: 1900

World Series championships: 1906, 1917, 2005

Team name: The White Sox got their name because white socks were part of the team's uniform. Most teams have at least three colors in their uniforms. But White Sox uniforms are just white and black.

Major League Baseball Web site for kids:
http://www.mlb.com/mlb/kids/

INDEX